BIRMINGHAM CITY
University

Please
remember to
return or
renew on time
to avoid fines

Renew/check due dates via
www.bcu.ac.uk/library

SCHOLASTIC

For ages **9 to 11**

Pie Corbett

Storyteller

Traditional tales to read, tell and write

Terms and conditions: CD-Rom

IMPORTANT – PERMITTED USE AND WARNINGS · READ CAREFULLY BEFORE USING

Minimum specification:
- PC or Mac with a 16x CD-Rom drive and 256 Mb RAM
- Windows 98 or higher
- Mac OS 10.1.5 to 10.6
- Recommended minimum processor speed: 800 MHz
- 16bit sound and graphics card

For all technical support queries, please phone Scholastic Customer Services on 0845 6039091.

Eight stories to watch on CD-Rom

Credits

'This series is dedicated to all those parents, storytellers and teachers who keep the flame of stories alive in children's minds.'
Pie Corbett

The publishers would like to thank the children and staff at Ebrington, Grasmere and South Grove Primary Schools for their help in creating this product.

Author
Pie Corbett

Editor
Sarah Snashall

Development Editors
Simret Brar / Rachel Mackinnon

Cover Illustration
© Gettyimages

Illustrations
© Ray and Corrine Burrows

Series Designer / Designer
Andrea Lewis

Cover Montage
Andrew Biscomb

CD-ROM Development
Q and D Multimedia Ltd / Adrian Moss/ Atmospheres Ltd

Text © 2008 Pie Corbett
© 2008 Scholastic Ltd

Designed using Adobe InDesign

Published by Scholastic Ltd
Book End
Range Road
Witney
Oxfordshire
OX29 0YD

www.scholastic.co.uk

Printed by Bell and Bain Ltd
13 14 15 16 17 18 19   6 7

British Library Cataloguing-in-Publication Data
A catalogue record for this book is available from the British Library.

ISBN 978-1407-10069-2

Acknowledgements
The publishers would like to thank **Patricia Leighton** for the use of *The Widow's Daughters* by Patricia Leighton © 2008, Patricia Leighton (2008, previously unpublished).

The right of the Pie Corbett to be identified as the author of this work has been asserted by him in accordance with the Copyright, Designs and Patents Act 1988.

Contents

For ages
9 to 11

*Three golden apples fall from heaven –
one is for the person who tells the tale;
one is for the person who listens;
and one is for the person who passes it on.*

About the series

Storyteller develops the spoken art of storytelling through print, audio, video and the spoken word. The series comprises for 9 to 11 year olds:

- *The Boy and the Tiger* – a collection of 15 stories with an audio CD (providing all the stories read aloud).
- *Storyteller Ages 9 to 11* – teacher's notes on each story with a CD-Rom (providing videos of eight stories being told and four storytellers talking about their craft).

The aim of *Storyteller* is to provide a bank of stories that families, teachers and children might retell and develop to make their own.

Why tell stories?

Storytelling weaves a spell that binds us all into one world community. We enter that other world where anything is possible and we can think, feel and grow together. They help us to fashion who we are and to know what is right and what is wrong.

Many schools have discovered that if children learn stories orally, it improves the quality of their writing. This is because oral storytelling develops the children's self-confidence as storytellers, it provides a bank of possibilities to draw upon and encourages the flow of story language and patterns that they can use when writing. If a child knows a story really well, when they sit down to write, it makes the task of writing easier because the brain does not have to compose at the same time as tackling handwriting, spelling and punctuation.

Research has shown that children who are read to and hear stories before coming to school are the most likely to succeed in school. This is because stories help children to sit still, listen and concentrate; they also develop abstract thinking so that children who have had stories told or read to them are the first to form abstract concepts across the curriculum. In addition, stories create a comforting and imaginative world in which ogres can be confronted and our deepest fears played out and controlled. The importance of story has been recognised in the new National Curriculum, which requires children to retell and be familiar with fairy stories, traditional tales, myths and legends from our literary heritage, other cultures and traditions.

As educationalists, we also know that children who are read to or have stories told to them begin to build up and internalise narrative possibilities. Through repetitive, memorable and meaningful storytelling, children build up:

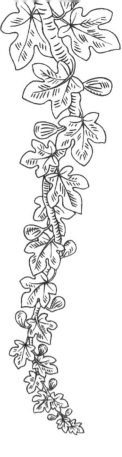

- **The big patterns of stories** – rather like putting templates in the mind. Ted Hughes called these 'blueprints for the imagination'.
- **The building blocks of a story** – openings, dilemmas, action, suspense, resolutions as well as characters, settings and events.
- **The flow of sentences** – because story sentences are different to everyday speech. For instance, *In a distant valley lived a giant*.
- **Words** – not only descriptive language and tricks such as alliteration or imagery – but also story language such as *once upon a time, one day, unfortunately, luckily* and *finally*.

The conditions for internalising these narrative patterns are as follows:

- **Repetition** – the stories have to be heard not once, not twice but at least three times. Children then need time to keep retelling their version in order to gain fluency and confidence.
- **Memorable** – the stories have to be made memorable so that they stay inside the child's mind, a metaphor for their lives. This is why in the teacher's notes I have provided suggestions for artwork, drama, and other forms of exploration.
- **Meaningful** – if the language of the story is to become generative then the children have to understand what the sentences mean. Again, this is why we might paint scenes, act the story out with puppets or hot-seat characters. All of these activities help children to deepen their understanding and appreciation – as well as ensuring that the patterns can be internalised and reused as part of the child's linguistic competence.
- **Hear it** – to internalise a story, it is important that children *hear* them. This may be through the audio CD, watching the videos on the CD-Rom or having the teacher read the story aloud – or most effectively, tell the story. A good telling creates the story in the child's mind.
- **Telling it** – to internalise the story so that it becomes their own, the children have to retell it. Language is learned by 'hearing it' and then 'saying it'. Of course, they will need time to retell a tale until they have gained fluency and confidence.

On the CD-Rom you will find:

Oral performances of eight stories:

1. *The Man in Search of his Luck* told by Pie Corbett
2. *Pumpkin* told by Xanthe Gresham
3. *The Fearsome Giant* told by Taffy Thomas
4. *Nyangara, the Fire Python* told by Jane Grell
5. *The Impossible Escape* told by Pie Corbett
6. *The Cobbler and the Dragon* told by Pie Corbett
7. *The Farmer's Fun-Loving Daughter* told by Taffy Thomas
8. *Cinderella* told by Pie Corbett

Storytellers talking about their craft:

Pie Corbett
Xanthe Gresham
Taffy Thomas
Jane Grell

How to tell a story

Telling a story yourself

Storytelling is not as daunting as one might first imagine. We all have a natural propensity towards telling and will have told many anecdotes and recounted many events. Make storytelling easier by following these tips:

- **Choose a story** – find a tale that you like. Start with something fairly brief that has a repetitive pattern.
- **Adapt the story** – this stage is not necessary, but it definitely helps to rewrite the story that you're going to tell because it helps internalise the pattern (and build in any specific language pattern that you want the children to learn).
- **Draw a story map, board or flowchart** – this is crucial. Annotate any rhythmic patterns or special words that you must use (though keep writing to a minimum). Any pictures will help you 'see' the story in your mind.
- **Listen to it** – use the audio CD (supplied with the anthology). Listen and then join in to gain confidence. Listening to the story at least three times in order to be able to attempt a retelling.
- **Try saying the story aloud** – you can have the map in front of you, or just try to see the story in your head. Practise telling the story several times on your own.
- **Now tell it** – find a class and retell the story. You will be surprised how easy it is. Remember that you do not have to know most of the stories word for word.

Cinderella Story Map

Illustration © Scholastic Ltd

Helping the children retell

Learning a story takes time. However, the more experienced the children become, the quicker they can learn. Storytelling improves memory. Help the children retell stories by following this process:

- **Listen to the story** – a number of times. Initially, tell the tale and then discuss likes, dislikes, puzzles and, patterns.
- **Draw a story map** – ask the children to listen to the story again and draw a story map or board or a flowchart of key scenes.
- **Watch it** – watch the story on the CD-Rom. Discuss with the children what they liked about 'how' the storytellers tell their tales. Make a list of criteria for good storytelling. For example: speak clearly and loudly; vary the volume, expresssion and pace; use gestures to support the meaning. It might be interesting to compare the written and told versions, which in some cases vary considerably.

- **Activities** – undertake other activities such as drama, writing in role, art, model making, and so on. Set up the audio CD in a listening corner.
- **Join in** – retell the story and encourage the children to increasingly join in. In the end, you may have a unique class version! (With children who have English as a new language or where children struggle with speaking, learning some 'communal' tales word for word can be very helpful. You will find that each anthology has some simple tales with repetitive patterns that would lend themselves to this form of retelling. It is crucial to help the children by using actions for the key events and connectives as well as the map.)
- **Use actions** – use actions with enthusiasm to enhance events.
- **Paired retellings** – put the children in pairs and ask them to retell the tale, either together or by taking turns (they can use their maps or flowcharts). Remember, they do not have to learn the story word for word – they are developing their own fluent retelling. The less confident should stick more closely to the original retelling; be wary of more confident children who may have a tendency to make the tale so elaborate that it loses impact.
- **Let pairs or individuals retell** – and ask the class to evaluate. In this way, children learn from each other.
- **Bit by bit** – with long stories, it can be helpful if children work on different sections of the story, bit by bit.
- **Perform** – when ready, ask the children to perform to other classes in pairs or individually; capture the performances on video or record on audio.
- **Writing** – finally, you may wish the children to move into writing. Use shared writing to show how the story may be crafted further as a precursor to the children's own writing.

Making the stories your own

Once children have a fluent version of the basic story, then you can begin to craft the tale. This can be done in various ways, from the simple to the complex. For example:

- Substitutions – change a few details such as names, places, animals and objects. Basically, it is the same story but only a few words altered.
- Addition – retell the story, making a few changes but adding more details, description, events or dialogue. Try not to let it get out of control!
- Alteration – try altering characters or settings or events so that there are consequences. The story stays within the overall frame but may veer in new directions. Try changing the ending or altering the sequence of events.
- Change of view – retell from a different angle (by a different character or as a diary, letter or news report).
- Recycle the plot – retell, but alter everything except for the underlying plot pattern or theme.

Precede writing a new version by drawing a new story map or flowchart. Allow plenty of chances to retell the new story. Model how to do this with a new class version, then let the children draw their own new story and retell. They will need to retell their story at least three times for it to begin to become fluent. Some children will need at least six retellings before writing.

The Man in Search of his Luck

About the story

This story is found in Greece and Bulgaria, as well as Iraq and India. There is also a Chinese version involving a dragon. In this Greek version, a man travels to see the Undying Sun rather than God. The French storyteller Abbi Patrix tells this story as part of a long sequence. It is a great story to tell because of the surprise ending and the rhythmic pattern.

Getting to know the story well

Read aloud or tell the story to the class. Use the following activities to help the children embed the key elements of the story prior to learning to tell it out loud.

Discuss

- Talk about the twist at the end of the story and the theme of the story: we all make our own luck. Discuss as a class the ways in which the man is stupid.
- Discuss which of the characters in the story are lucky and which unlucky? Is the man lucky to have love and wealth offered to him; or is he unlucky to be so stupid? Is the lion the only lucky character or is he the only one that makes his luck?

Drama

- Hot-seat the man's friends or relations. Encourage the children to ask questions about the man that directly feed into his character in the story: his temperament, his luck and his stupidity?
- Interview the man at the point where he finds there is some luck. Can the child playing the man capture his excitement?
- Hot-seat the sad girl. Freeze-frame at the moment where he talks to her the second time and interview them both.

Story behind the story

- Can the children create a story that ends with the treasure chest under the tree? Challenge then to tell a scene in which it is discovered.
- In a different tone, ask the children to tell the tragic story of the lonely girl. Ask them to imagine how the story ends – does she finally meet someone to marry?
- Ask the children to invent a comedy scene in which the man is so unlucky he decides it's time to search for his luck.

Retelling the story aloud

- Ask the children to recount the key scenes in the story.
- The flowchart breaks down the story into its key components. Talk through the structure of the story with the class pointing out how the repetitive structure helps the storyteller. Draw a story map for the story (see page 6).
- This story is good for retelling in pairs, with pairs of children working on different scenes. Ask each pair to build description and characterisation. When the pairs are ready, display the flowchart and ask the pairs to retell their scene in turn.
- This is a good story for practising some oral storytelling techniques.

In their pairs, ask the children to:
- speed up on the linking sections;
- slow down at the dramatic point with the lion;
- lower and raise voice according to meaning;
- use dramatic pause for the comic ending.

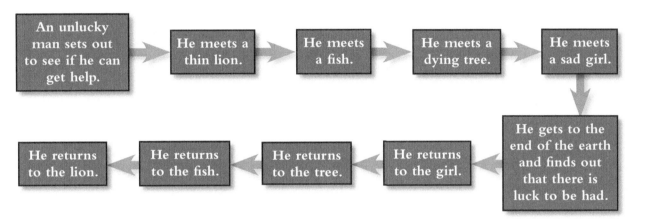

From telling to writing

- When the children are confident enough with the oral retelling of their paired section, ask them to write it down. Build in specific challenges, such as:
  - Use an 'adverb starter' to show how the man feels when he sees the lion, fish, tree and girl, for example: *'Cautiously, he stepped forwards…'*
  - Build the description of the lion, fish, tree or the girl, for example: *'The tree's branches were thin and spindly. The leaves were brown and already had fallen to the ground, even though it was summer. The tree's bark was peeling off and it creaked in the wind like an old man.'*
  - Reveal how the girl feels by showing more of what she is thinking, for example: *'She sniffed and thought back to when…'*
  - Work on the dialogue so that children rehearse a simple pattern.
- Set some children the challenge of writing a new version of the story. They might like the challenge of having a woman, girl or boy as the main character. What forms would their luck take? The trick ending has to stay pretty much the same, although a different animal than a lion might be interesting – a bear for instance. How about resetting the story in modern times, a forest or a 'futuristic' city?

Six Go Through the World

About the story
This story is of eastern European origin and a longer version is found in *The Complete Grimm's Fairy Tales*. Daniel Morden's retelling is faithful to the original, but much sparser and more rhythmic, which makes it ideal for oral retelling. Daniel Morden writes, 'There are many different versions of it- The Bremen Town Musicians, Jason and the Argonauts, The Magnificent Seven, even The X Men are all variants.

Getting to know the story well
Read aloud or tell the story to the class. Use the following activities to help the children embed the key elements of the story prior to learning to tell it.

Drama
- Hot-seat different characters from the story to find out what they think about the thief.
- Hot seat the man with two sets of knees, the man with the enormous eye, the white man, the burly man and the blowing man. How do they feel about their unusal gifts. Hot seat them again at the end of the story – how do their feelings differ?
- Organise the children in pairs and ask them to practise: 'smiling with their mouth, but not their eyes'.
- Ask the children to act out a village scene and, as villagers, gossip about what might be going to happen in the race.
- Work in groups with the children taking on the characters of the six men and role play what happened when they entered the room that turned out to be an oven.

Writing in role
- Write and design the poster that was nailed to a tree. Make a list of extraordinary things the thief might have stolen, including sounds and tastes, starting with 'The miraculous thief stole…'. In role as journalists, interview the runner, the Princess, the King and the marksman. Write a 150-word newspaper article about the race.

Story behind the story
- In pairs, invent the possible other stories for the strange men.
- Read the Grimm's version of the story and compare it with Daniel Morden's version – what are the key differences?

Retelling the story aloud

With the class, work out the underlying pattern of the story.

- The flow chart breaks down the story into its key components.

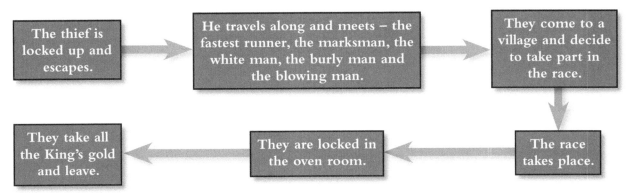

- In pairs, ask the children to use the flow chart and story maps to practise retelling the story, working on different sections of the story at a time. Remind them that they do not have to know it word for word – embellishments can add to the original.
- Daniel Morden writes:
  - "Make a feature of the repeated phrases or they will become tiresome. Acknowledge that the audience knows what the thief is about to say. Invite them to join in with the Thief when he says 'Tell us of yourself' and 'I could do with one such as you. Come with us and we'll make our fortune'."
  - "Go to town with the physical characteristics of the six friends. Describe them in detail. Employ gesture, facial expressions to make each of the friends larger than life."

From telling to writing

- Encourage embellishment of the original story. In this version the princess only plays a small part – can the children develop a stronger role for her? Perhaps there is some love interest? Does she get on with the King? In the Grimm's version, the soldier is only given a farthing for fighting in the war and sets out to take revenge on the King. Try using this idea to add to the thief's motives.
- Set the children specific tasks to alter or embellish the story, for example using characterisation, and dialogue.
- In a shared writing session, rewrite the story with more detail. Slow the pace of the telling so that the words can be crafted:

  The door swung open. To the King's amazement, the six were still standing. He had expected them to be roasted, but instead they were stamping their feet and shivering. Icicles hung from the ceiling like silvery teeth. Frost glittered on the floor. Snow powdered the tapestries like icing sugar…

Pumpkin

About the story

This story has a simplicity and charm. It has similarities with 'Billy Goats Gruff' in that the main character delays being eaten up by promising something better will eventually come along.

Getting to know the story well

Read aloud, watch, or tell the story to the class. Use the following activities to help the children embed the key elements of the story prior to learning to tell it out loud.

> **Watch it**
> Watch this story being told by Xanthe Gresham on the CD-Rom.

Drama

- Hot-seat the animals to see what they have to say about what happened. The children might enjoy interviewing the animals in role as a police officer who is investigating a report that people have been threatened while walking through the forest.

Writing in role

- Write as journalists about the extraordinary event of the rolling pumpkin. This could also be done as a short television news bulletin – you could film the children (remember to get parents' or carers' permission before filming the children). The old woman is good at getting out of dodgy situations with a simple excuse.

- Make a class list of 'excuses for not being eaten up' – these could include 'I'm only skin and bones', 'My skin is made of plastic', or 'I'm on the way to the pie shop and will be fatter on the way back'.

Art

- Bring in some pumpkins or other gourds. Hollow these out to make pumpkin soup. Then carve faces and put candles into the pumpkins.

Retelling the story out loud

- Spend time watching Xanthe Gresham tell the story on the CD-Rom. What do the children notice about 'how' she tells the story? Explore the use of pause, the varying of pace and of course, her use of sound effects and expression. Practise copying how she tells the story.

- This story is ideal for communal retelling, as most of it is sufficiently patterned to be learned by heart by simple listening and joining in until the children know the tale well enough to retell it on their own.

- This story is also ideal for a group retelling, using a narrator and others to play the lady, her daughter, the various creatures and her two dogs. It could be presented as a play – with the narrator telling the story while it is enacted. Key Stage 1 children would make a perfect audience.
- The flowchart breaks down the story into its key components. Display the flowchart to aid the children as well as drawing story maps (see page 6).

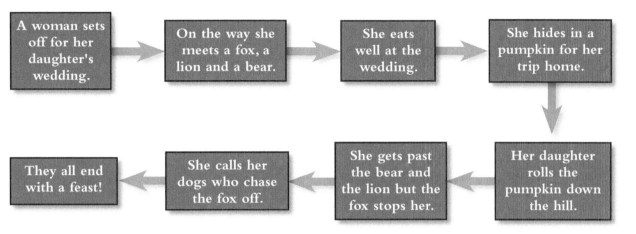

A woman sets off for her daughter's wedding. → On the way she meets a fox, a lion and a bear. → She eats well at the wedding. → She hides in a pumpkin for her trip home. ↓ Her daughter rolls the pumpkin down the hill. ← She gets past the bear and the lion but the fox stops her. ← She calls her dogs who chase the fox off. ← They all end with a feast!

- Xanthe Gresham writes: "Many storytellers walk their story in. They use their steps to make the rhythm and they keep it simple so that they can remember it. Many years ago storytellers sang their stories and this is what you are doing when you walk your story. You are dancing the story into yourself so that you don't just remember it with your brain. You remember it with your body and the intonations of your voice. It stays fresh because if you walk you have to breathe in and out and remember where you are going." As a class, have a go at walking up and down whilst telling parts of the story. Do the children find that this helps the remember the story and to tell it with rhythm?

From telling to writing

When the children are ready, encourage them to write down their own version.
- This story is ideal for turning into a simple picture book for younger children – a zigzag book would work well. Work with the children to create a simple storyboard of the main scenes with the text written underneath. Alternatively the children could paint the main scenes and then take photographs of these to create a slideshow presentation of the story, picture by picture. Once this is done, the children can add in their writing to accompany each slide.
- Challenge some children to write a version of the story in a contemporary setting. On a journey the main character is threatened, but manages to escape. Fearing what will happen on the way back, the main character plans to wear a disguise or hide inside a car or lorry in order to escape and get back home.

The Boy and the Tiger

About the story

Daniel Morden heard this story in the rural north of Haiti. It is a good story for provoking debate, and a good excuse to bring some figs into the classroom!

Getting to know the story well

After sharing the story with the children, use the following activities to embed the key elements.

Discuss

- Hold a class debate about justice. Why did the boy have the monkey chased away – can the children think of any reasons for this, or do they feel it was unjust?
- Ask: are people as cruel as this story suggests?

Art

- Look at pictures of tigers' fur. Provide materials for the children to create patterns using vivid orange and black.

Story behind the story

- Challenge the children to tell the story of how the tiger got into the hole in the first place.
- What about the story of what happens to the boy next?

Retelling the story aloud

- Notice how trimmed back this story has become through constant retelling. It is a good story to learn together. Following that, the children can flesh it out, adding detail, such as characterisation, setting and more description of the action without detracting from the pace of the plot.
- Display the flowchart for the story and also set the children to drawing their own story map (see page 6).

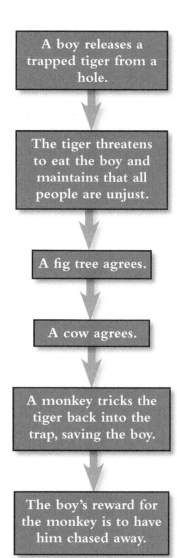

A boy releases a trapped tiger from a hole.

The tiger threatens to eat the boy and maintains that all people are unjust.

A fig tree agrees.

A cow agrees.

A monkey tricks the tiger back into the trap, saving the boy.

The boy's reward for the monkey is to have him chased away.

From telling into writing

- Following the class debate, in a shared writing session change the ending of the written story, to one that reflects the children's own sense of justice.
- More confident writers could use the themes of 'justice' and 'fairness' to create a new story in which the main character helps someone in trouble who then turns on them.

Aldar-Kose's Cloak

Getting to know the story

After sharing the story with the children, use the following activities to help the children embed the key elements prior to telling it.

Discuss

- Compare this story to 'Ragamuffin and his Delicious Nail Soup'. How are the main characters and plot similar? Most cultures have a 'trickster' figure who outwits the others. What other examples are there in folktales?
- Ask: why does Aldar-Kose not take the man's money?

Story behind the story

- As a class, create a story of how the rich man plays the same trick on someone else.

Retelling the story

- This story is a good early tale because it is simple to learn. Chant the opening rhythmically.
- The flowchart breaks down the story into its key components.
- Helen East writes, "I imagine Aldar-Kose cool and calm, lolling in his saddle, so I usually lean back in my chair when I tell for him, wheras the rich man, by contrast I make all jittery and twitchy, eager to grab a bargain. That affects how their voices come out." Ask the children to try out Helen East's techniques.
- Once learned, the story could be embellished by claiming that the cloak has magical properties that keep it warm. Build up the beginning to emphasize how cold Aldar-Kose is and how slowly his horse travels.

From telling into writing

- Try modernising the story with a modern trickster who manages to gain something by deceit.

Aldar-Kose is travelling in threadbare clothes and on an old horse.

⬇

A rich man passes by and Aldar-Kose starts singing happily.

⬇

The man asks why he is so happy when he has so little.

⬇

Aldar-Kose claims his cloak is special and keeps him warm.

⬇

The rich man asks if he can buy the cloak.

⬇

Aldar-Kose tricks the rich man out of his cloak and the horse.

The Fearsome Giant

About the story

This story is popular with storytellers. There are many tales of characters facing their fear and in Grimm's tales there is the story of a boy who went in search of his fear. It is similar to 'The Monster over the Hill' retold by Daniel Morden in *Dragonory and Other Stories* and provides an interesting example of how a story can be dressed up in many ways but still hold the same underlying truth.

Getting to know the story

Read aloud, watch, or tell the story to the class. Use the following activities to help the children embed the key elements of the story prior to learning to tell it out loud.

> **Watch it**
> Watch this story being told by Taffy Thomas on the CD-Rom.

Discuss

■ Discuss with the children what they think this story is really about? Can the children see the story as a parable about fear?

■ Ask: what was the King really afraid of? What about the people? Did the giant really shrink? Why did knowing the giant's name help? Where was the fear?

■ Explain that the hen-wife is the 'helper' – a character that often appears in stories to assist the main character, such as Cinderella's 'fairy godmother'. Create a class list of 'helpers' from stories that they know. Understanding such characters as types can help the children in their retelling.

Drama

■ Ask a group of children to role play the people going to see the King and begging him to do something about the giant. Remind the children that the King is afraid of being in charge and that the people are afraid of having a new king.

■ Ask children to work in pairs to role play the conversation between the young, scared King and the wise hen-wife.

Dance

■ Set the giant's chant to percussive music and with the children create a simple stomping dance to accompany it.

Story behind the story

■ Ask the children to tell the stories that spread quickly about the giant that are referred to at the start of the tale. These could be told from the point of view of a traveller on the journey who meets the giant or sees its shadow or hears its chant. Encourage the children to go to town with dramatic details as the traveller exaggerates the tale.

Retelling the story aloud

- Prepare the children for telling the story themselves by watching Taffy Thomas tell the story on the CD-Rom. Pick up on his dramatic techniques.
- This is a meaty version of the story and will need plenty of retelling and listening in order to gain fluency and confidence. Nonetheless, the effort is worthwhile. The more it is told, drawn, discussed, organised, listened to and watched, the more likely the children will be able to retell the tale.
- Start with the structure of the story. Work with the class to create a flowchart of the key events. You will end up with something like the flowchart below.
- Organise the children to work in groups. Ask them to divide up the boxes in the flowchart between them with each member of the group working on a retelling of part of the story.
- More confident children can work on telling more and more of the story until they can tell the whole story.
- Display the flowchart and a story map that you have created with the children to help them to keep on track when retelling the story.

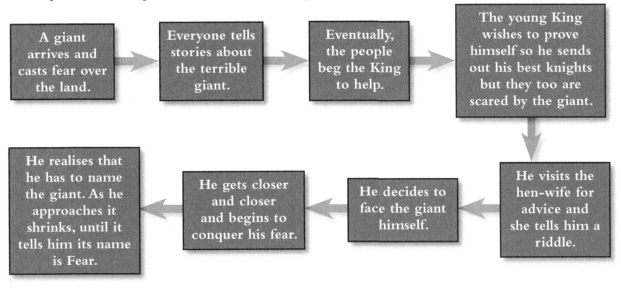

From telling to writing

- Once the children have developed a fluent oral retelling, writing a version of this story would make a good extended writing project.
- Use shared writing sessions to help the children craft their stories in a more literary fashion. It helps to personalise the story by using names for the characters and by fleshing out descriptions to add drama and so that the events seem real. For example:

  King Gudrun took a pace forwards and then halted. He could hear a low grinding noise and the sound of stones moving. A dark shadow had begun to tower above him and the pony whinnied. His heart thumped and he could feel his fists clench tighter on the reins. He shook his head, dismounted and left the pony...

Nyangara, the Fire Python

About the story

This story fits the story tradition of wisdom overcoming strength. In many stories, including 'The Fearsome Giant', above, the strongest characters fail an ordeal, then the weakest character succeeds through charm, cunning or bravery.

Getting to know the story

Read aloud, watch, or tell the story to the class. Use the following activities to help the children embed the key elements of the story prior to learning to tell it out loud.

Watch it
Watch this story being told by Jane Grell on the CD-Rom.

Discuss

- Discuss the character of Amoafi and how her feelings change through the story. Draw a character graph showing how her feelings change from worry about her father to fear on the journey to elation when she has succeeded in her task. Discuss how Jane Grell captures these feelings as she tells the story.

- Ask: why is fire so precious that people still tell stories about it? What would fire have meant to the villagers who first told this story? Can the children name any other stories about fire?

- Ask: who in the story is the strongest or the bravest? What sorts of strength are there? Discuss with the class how the story sets up the expectation that it is the men not the women who are suitable for such tasks. Compare this with the young defenseless king beating the giant in 'The Fearsome Giant', where the soldiers have failed.

Drama

- Organise children to work in groups of four to role play a television journalist interviewing the chief's three sons.

- Ask for a volunteer to take on the role of Amoafi. Hot-seat Amoafi at the beginning and at the end of the story.

Music and dance

- Set the song Amoafi sings to Nyangara to a simple melody. Use chime bars and gentle percussion and learn this as a group or class. Try retelling the story with the musical background.

Retelling the story

- Watch this story on the CD-Rom. Ask the children to observe and comment on how Jane Grell tells the story.
- As a class, remember the key elements of the story. Develop the discussion to create a flowchart of the key events. You will end up with something like the this:

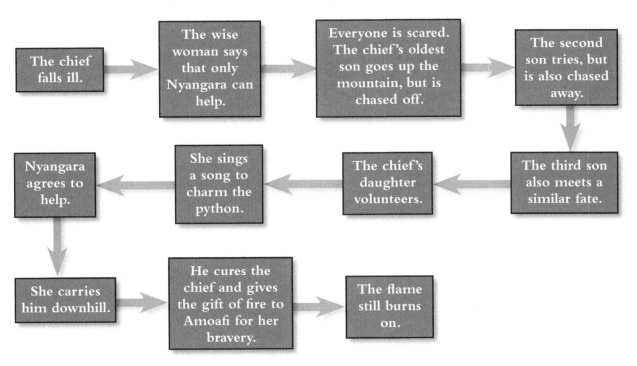

- Encourage the children to start with the bare bones of the story as outlined in the flowchart and then to embellish the story with each retelling. Creating a story map (see page 6) before telling also helps.

From telling to writing

- Before writing out their whole story, challenge the children to take the sentence, 'up to this day no one knows just how she managed this heavy burden down the mountainside' from Jane Grell's written version of this story, and to try writing this missing section of the story. For example:

  The python slithered around her neck and Amoafi could feel its dry skin, cool against her flesh. It coiled its way around her neck and over her arms till she felt its weight like a heavy sack. It rested its huge head on her shoulder, its black eyes staring at her like twin beads and its tongue flickering. Step by step, she began the long climb down...

- Challenge more confident writers to write their own tale about someone who tries to get something which is needed - perhaps water. At first the strong ones try but fail – then the weaker one overcomes any obstacles.

Regrets and The Impossible Escape

Getting to know the story

Read aloud, watch, or tell the stories to the class. Present the stories as riddles and see if the children can guess what will happen before revealing the endings.

Watch it
Watch 'The Impossible Escape' being told by Pie Corbett on the CD-Rom.

Discuss

- Talk about the ending of 'Regrets'. Ask: would it be possible to avoid having regrets in the story? Is possible to live without regret? What sorts of things do the children regret?

Drama

- Interview characters from either story.
- Choose children to freeze-frame the moment of decision-making in the Land of Darkness in 'Regrets' for the rest of the class. Ask the children to turn to a partner and discuss what the men and women should do? Send one of the characters from the freeze-frame down a conscience alley, to see whether they should take the pebbles or not.

Writing in role

- Write a message from someone in 'Regrets' suggesting what others entering the Land of Darkness should do.
- Make a list of possible ways to escape from a magical prison. For example: Sprout wings and fly high; shrink to the size of a pea and squeeze through the lock; become invisible and slip through a wall; slim yourself down and slip between the bars.

Art

- Draw or paint the Land of Darkness – what sorts of creatures might be glimpsed there?
- Produce cartoon versions of the tales.

Retelling the story aloud

■ The short nature of these stories makes them ideal starting points for first time storytellers. Both can be learnt word-for-word.

■ Simple maps or cartoons could be drawn and used to rehearse retellings, or display a flowchart of the stories to give the children confidence.

Regrets

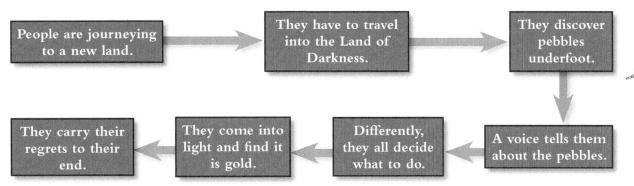

People are journeying to a new land. → They have to travel into the Land of Darkness. → They discover pebbles underfoot.

They carry their regrets to their end. ← They come into light and find it is gold. ← Differently, they all decide what to do. ← A voice tells them about the pebbles.

The Impossible Escape

The man is put into prison. → He discovers that the prison is impossible to escape from. → Twenty minutes later he is free. → How did he manage this? → The explanation is given.

From telling to writing

■ Challenge the children to turn 'Regrets' into a more fully formed story by extending each part of the tale, adding description and naming the characters. Rather than recounting what happened, actually tell the story. For example:

> *As they began to climb down into the Land of Darkness, the tunnel grew darker. Mica held his torch high and the flame flickered. Shadows moved among the rocks. He could hear the others, stumbling and muttering behind him.*
>
> *Where the tunnel ended, Mica could see that they were about to enter a large cavern. At that moment, a gust of wind blew and his torch went out. They were in total darkness. The cavern echoed as they trudged in. Mica could feel a strange pebbly surface underfoot. It was like walking on marbles. He stooped down and picked some up. They felt smooth.*
>
> *As they stood there, a voice came to them. A deep, husky whisper that sent a chill through the little band of companions. 'Welcome,' hissed the voice...*

The Widow's Daughters

Getting to know the story

Read aloud or tell the story and the poem to the class.

Discuss

- Ask the children to note down what we know about the characters from what they say and do. Rate their 'goodness' on a scale from one to ten.
- Discuss what the story is about – what can we learn from the story? Do the children feel that the ending is fair?
- Compare the poem and the story – what are the advantages of each format? Which do the children prefer?

Drama

- With the class, role play the opening of the story with the old woman on her own, muttering to herself and feeling weaker and weaker – perhaps wondering where her children are and what they are doing.
- Role play the scenes where the three daughters are visited by the squirrel. Freeze-frame each scene and interview the characters to see what they are thinking and to explore why they behave as they do.
- Set children to role play a telephone conversation between the daughters.

Art

- Use images from the internet to create simple designs of a tortoise, spider and bee. Use these to illustrate written versions of the story.

Retelling the story aloud

- Organise the children to work in pairs to learn the poem by heart and to practise a performance of the poem. Encourage them to work on creating a sense of drama with the squirrel's curses to the two daughters.
- More able children might like to attempt a retelling of the story rather than the poem. Create a flowchart to help structure their retellings.

The widow's daughters get married and leave home.

↓

The squirrel finds her sick, runs for help, but the first daughter is busy cleaning her bowl.

↓

The second daughter is too busy weaving cloth.

↓

The third daughter leaves her bread-making and comes running.

↓

The daughter comforts her mother as she dies.

↓

The daughters become a tortoise a spider and a bee respectively.

The Widow's Daughters

There was a poor widow
who had three daughters
fair as the flowers and bright as the sun
and hard she worked
and long she worked
to feed and keep each one.

The three fair daughters
Found three good husbands
and one by one they went
and the lonely widow
carried on working
'til all her strength was spent.

A squirrel found her
sick and dying,
huddled and cold in her bed.
'Hurry, my friend,
to my three fair daughters.
Fetch them home,' she said.

The squirrel raced off
to her eldest daughter.
'Hurry, your mother is dying, poor soul.'
'I'll come, of course,'
said the widow's daughter,
'but first I must finish cleaning this bowl.'

'Your bowl!
Your bowl!'
cried the angry squirrel.
'Live forever
in your bowl!'

The squirrel raced off to the second daughter.
'Hurry, hurry before she is dead!'
'I would come at once
but I'm so, so busy.
I must weave this cloth for the fair,' she said.

'Weave what?
Weave cloth!'
cried the angry squirrel.
'Weave on, wicked daughter,
and never stop.'

He came at last
to the third fair daughter
mixing and fixing dough for her bread.
When she heard his news
she rushed from the house
and ran and ran to her mother's bed.

'You will bring joy,'
said the squirrel,
'wherever you go, sweet friend,
and people will love you
for ever and ever
'til the world itself shall end.'

So what became of the widow's daughters
fair as fair could be?
What became of those daughters
one — two — three?

The first turned into a tortoise,
the second a spider became
but the third brought sweetness to all the world
and honey bee is her name.

Patricia Leighton

From telling to writing

■ Retell a new version of the story using the theme of not helping others. This could be set in a modern setting, for example:

Sandi looked out of the window at the old lady at the bus stop. The rain was driving hard and she looked soaked. Already two buses had driven straight past. Sandi knew that she should let her shelter in the warm, but the shelves had to be filled and then she had to tidy the storeroom ...

The Cobbler and the Dragon

About the story

This is probably the best-known legend that children know in Poland. It tells the story of how the city of Krakow was named.

Getting to know the story

Read aloud, watch, or tell the story to the class. Use the following activities to help the children embed the key elements of the story prior to learning to tell it out loud.

Watch it
Watch this story being told by Pie Corbett on the CD-Rom.

Discuss

- Many stories have a monster or fierce creature that threatens people. Many have a small, weak or unlikely character who turns out to be strong. Can the children recall any other stories with these elements? ('The Fearsome Giant' and 'Nyangara' would be good comparisons).
- Ask: why would such stories prove to be popular? Why do they appeal to most people?

Drama

- As a class, role play the market square with the children as stallholders and shoppers, discussing rumours about missing animals, various princes who have tried to defeat the dragon, sightings of the dragon, and now the rumour that the King is having to give up his daughter.
- Enact how the cobbler hears about the need for a dragon slayer and then the scene where he is brought before the King.
- Role play a few farmers seeing the end of the story happening with the dragon flying to the river.

Writing in role

- Design posters advertising for someone to defeat the dragon. (Wanted: Dragon Slayer. Must be able to…).
- Ask the children to write a set of instructions: How to defeat a dragon.

Art

- Paint or make a papier-mâché model of the dragon.

Research

- Locate Poland and Krakow on a map of Europe – if possible, use the internet to find a map of the city showing the river Vistula.
- Investigate other dragon stories for retelling.

Retelling the story aloud

- This is a fairly simple story to retell and does not have to be learned word for word. Help the children get to know the story well by watching the video on the CD-Rom a few times.
- Create a flowchart for the story with the class (you'll end up with something like the flowchart below) or ask the children to draw a story map (see page 6). Display the flowchart or story maps as the children plan their retellings.
- Ask the children to take time in pairs to build up a retelling so that they become fluent storytellers, using story maps or boards.

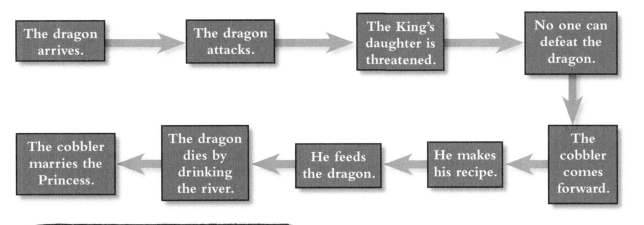

From telling to writing

- This would make a good story to embellish because there are scenes missing. For instance, the scene where the cobbler hears about what is happening and decides to visit the King is not told. Begin by orally developing the plot, adding in description to flesh out the tale. Work on building characterisation of the cobbler and the King. Add in the Princess – or take her out of the tale and provide a reward instead. Construct descriptions of the settings and action. Build suspense as the cobbler approaches the lair. For example:

  Krak paused at the edge of the cave. He could smell the stench of rotting flesh. From somewhere inside the cavern, he could hear a low rumbling and the crunch of stones as the dragon shifted its vast belly. He stepped inside and almost immediately the darkness closed around him. Step by step he moved closer till in the end he could see its huge shape, scales glinting and he could smell the sulphur as it breathed steam. Its eyes were closed…

- An interesting alternative would be to invent a story that tells the tale of how a place local to the school came to be named. Use a map or atlas to find a name that lends itself to such a tale. What other sorts of monsters might live near a local place and need defeating – dragons, ogres, giants, hobgoblins, snakes… Then decide how it can be defeated. Basically, this means retelling the same tale, 'conquering the monster', but using a new setting and creature and hero or heroine.

Ragamuffin and his Delicious Nail Soup

Getting to know the story

Use the following activities to embed the story prior to telling.

Discuss

■ Ask: is the tramp is 'wily' and a 'liar'? Could the old lady be described in the same way? Does she deserve her fate?

Drama

■ Orgnanise the children to role play the woman gossiping to a neighbour about what happened.

■ Role play the first time she uses the nail to make some soup.

Retelling the story aloud

■ This story can be pared right down when the children are ready to retell. Organise for the children to draw a story map (see page 6) for the story before they start.

■ Once they confident in their telling, encourage them to embellish or change the story as they wish. Tell them to go to town with the two characters as they try to trick each other.

The tramp arrives at the cottage.

He begins to make nail soup.

He asks for more and more ingredients.

They eat the soup.

The next day he sells the old woman the nail.

From telling to writing

■ When writing, build up the tramp's character more by adding in description. For example: *He paused and gave her a sideways glance. His eyes narrowed as he stirred the pot and took just the slightest sip…*

■ Show the children how to vary sentence openings for effect:
   adverb starters: *Carefully, he popped the nail into the soup…*
   'ing' or 'ed' starters: *Shaking her head, she scuttled off…*
   prepositional starters: *Into the pot, he dropped the potatoes…*
   time starters: *First, he asked her for…;*
   simile starters: *Quick as a tick, he…*

The Farmer's Fun-Loving Daughter

About the story

I know a version of this story from Ethiopia that is told as a riddle. In that version, three sons have to fill a room. The first son tries using straw, the second tries feathers and the third lights a candle and the light fills the room. Of course, there are many other stories in which people have to fulfil tasks. Often it is the third child – the laziest or silliest – who wins in the end. Before watching the story, it may be worth explaining what a 'will' is and the job of a lawyer.

Getting to know the story

Read aloud, watch, or tell the story to the class. Use the following activities to help the children embed the key elements of the story prior to learning to tell it out loud.

Watch it
Watch this story being told by Taffy Thomas on the CD-Rom.

Discuss

- Challenge the children to come up with other ways of filling a room. Use favourite ideas later when retelling the story.
- Do the children think that the outcome of the story is fair? Would it be fair of the girl to keep the farm for herself? Would she be the best farmer?

Drama

- As a class, hot seat the father and interview him about his will. Why does he think this is a good way to pass on his farm? Who does he think will inherit?
- Ask the children to role play in groups of four the scene where the lawyer reads the will and explains it to the farmer's three children.

Writing in role

- Ask the children to write the will. Talk about legal language and challenge the children to make the will as formal as possible. An internet search should provide correct phrases to incorporate.

Music

- Bring in a flute or play some flute music to the class.

Story behind the story

- Tell the story of what happened next. Did the farmer's daughter keep the farm for herself, or did she set a riddle or two for her brothers to win the farm?

Retelling the story

- This story is really an extended riddle. It would be useful to teach it alongside 'Regrets' and 'The Impossible Escape'. As it is a fairly simple story to retell, it would give confidence to less experienced storytellers. However, riddles do need careful telling as the wording can be important so the children should work in pairs or smallish groups to develop a fluent retelling of their own.
- Watch the story being told on the CD-Rom.
- The flowchart breaks down the story into its key components.

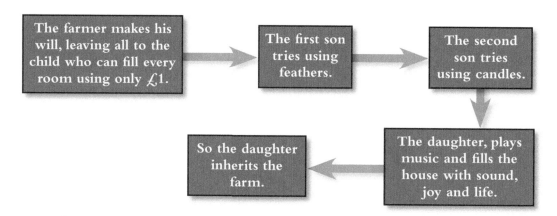

From telling into writing

- As a class project, create a book of riddles and include some retellings of this story. You might like to include 'Regrets' and 'The Impossible Escape'. Ask the children to interview their family and grandparents to collect some riddles. Of course, many children will know some themselves.
- When the children are ready to start writing their version of the story, explain that they do not have to have exactly the same answers but need to stick to the basic underlying pattern of the challenge – to fill the room with something. Might the ending be changed? Was there any reason that the boys deserved to be cut out of the inheritance?

  The farmer's fun-loving daughter decided to share the farm with her brothers. While she was the most cunning and spread happiness wherever she travelled, she knew that getting up at six in the morning to milk the cows was not something that she would enjoy! So in the end, everyone was happy and they are sure their father would have been pleased that greed had not stepped in between his children. Maybe, that was the real test after all?

Bella and the Bear

About the story

This story is well-known in Europe and there are various versions found in Russia and Scandinavia.

Getting to know the story

Read aloud or tell the story to the class. Use the following activities to help the children embed the key elements of the story prior to learning to tell it.

Discuss

- What other story does this remind the children of? In what way is the story like 'Little Red Riding Hood'?
- How does Bella manage to persuade the bear? Re-read carefully or listen again and list how she gradually manages to get her own way.
- Contrast the characters of Bella and the bear – gather clues that suggest their different persona.

Drama

- As a class, hot-seat the parents, the bear and finally Bella.
- Role play the scene when Bella left home to pick berries; role play the scene when her parents discover her hiding in the basket.
- Ask the children to develop a monologue for Bella, showing what thoughts were running her head when she lay in the basket overnight.

Writing in role

- Ask the children to create a list of 'ways to escape being trapped in a bear's den'. Capture the best ideas for writing a new version of the story.
- Challenge the children to write in role as Bella or the bear. Ask them to write a diary entry to recount what happened and they felt.
- Design a Wanted! or Warning! poster about the bear.

Story behind the story

- Tell the story of 'what happened next' to the bear. How will he try to outwit another child? How will the next child escape?

Retelling the story aloud

- When the children are familiar enough with the story and are ready to start telling it themselves, it might be useful to make a list of different ways of opening and ending stories. These 'formula' help to tune the audience and the teller into a story mood, breaking from reality so that a story world can be entered.

- This tale is ideal to retell in threes – a narrator, bear and Bella. Organise the children into groups of three and ask them to plan out their part of the story before starting to retell in a group. When the children are fluent in their retelling, organise for them to perform it to small groups in other classes.
- The flowchart breaks the story into key components. Use it to create a story map to use for retelling (see page 6).

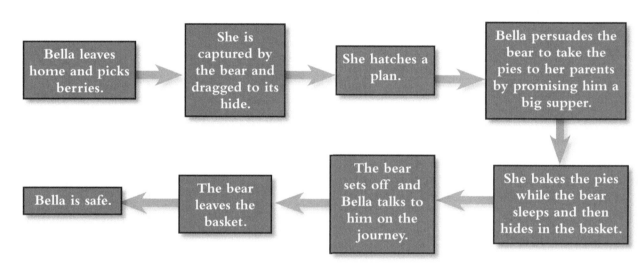

| Bella leaves home and picks berries. | She is captured by the bear and dragged to its hide. | She hatches a plan. | Bella persuades the bear to take the pies to her parents by promising him a big supper. |

| Bella is safe. | The bear leaves the basket. | The bear sets off and Bella talks to him on the journey. | She bakes the pies while the bear sleeps and then hides in the basket. |

From telling to writing

- This story would make an interesting mixture of prose and pictures in a written retelling. Most of the tale could be in prose, but some scenes could be shown as a mini cartoon across or down the page.
- To deepen the intensity of the tale, build up the threat of the bear by using suspense techniques and description to show that he is dangerous. For example:

  Bella stared at the bear. It towered above her. Its fierce red eyes glaring malevolently. She shuddered as it stretched out a paw towards her. She could see its yellow fangs. Spit dribbled from its great jaws that opened and closed like a vice.

- Alternatively, retell the story using the underlying theme of escape from a kidnap. Introduce a character who is kidnapped, tricks the kidnappers and escapes, returning home.

Cinderella

About the story

The story of Cinderella is probably the most widespread story. There are versions in virtually every part of the world. This version is based upon several English versions, recorded over a hundred years ago. When I was a child, my father read the story as retold by Joseph Jacobs so there are echoes of his retelling. This version has the mother returning in the form of a bird in role as 'fairy godmother'. In many versions, the ending is rather gruesome with the sisters trimming their feet and often having their eyes pecked out! Whilst the tale is very sad in parts, the ending is a triumph with Cinderella blossoming at the end and finding happiness whilst her oppressors get their just deserts.

Getting to know the story

Read aloud, watch, or tell the story to the class. Use the following activities to help the children embed the key elements of the story prior to learning to tell it out loud.

Watch it
Watch this story being told by Pie Corbett on the CD-Rom.

Discuss

■ Talk about the father and discuss what sort of ending might be suitable for him!

■ Watch the video of Cinderella on the CD-Rom. Compare this with the written version in the anthology. When I tell the story on the video, I elaborate and alter the tale's details in the course of retelling. What can the children learn from the retelling that they could use in their own oral version of the tale?

Art

■ Design Cinderella's dress and slippers for the ball.

Drama

■ Let the sisters and the step mother try to defend their behaviour in the hot seat. Put the father on trial for negligence.

Research

■ Compare this told version of Cinderella with the pantomime version of the story or other versions they might know. Draw up a list of similarities and differences.

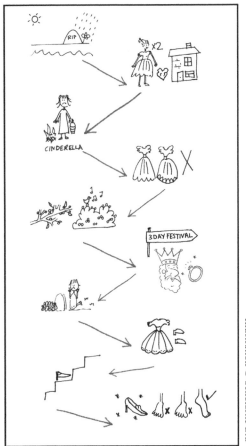

Retelling the story

- This is a more challenging story to tell. The children will need to tackle it in sections, working on a fluent retelling of each part. They do not have to know it word for word but should develop their own telling.
- Prepare the children by watching the video three of four times. Discuss the structure of the story and set the children to drawing their own story map (see page 6) of the story to use when their ready to start telling it.

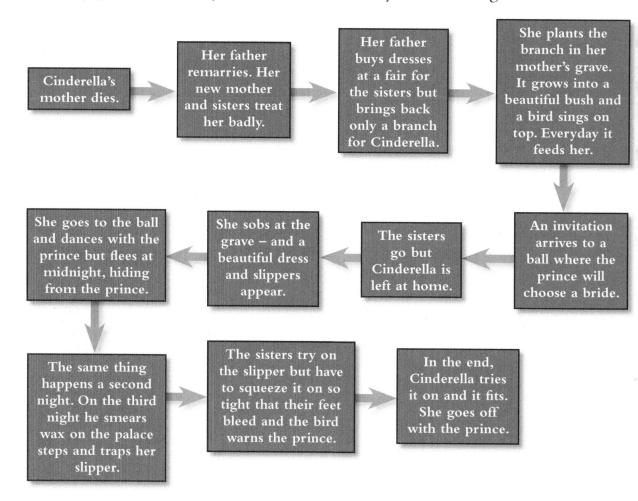

From telling into writing

- The children might find it fun to try to write a modern version of the story. This might be about a child who is mistreated by others but in the end gets a 'helper' on their side. The beginning of the film "James and the Giant Peach' is useful to watch as James is a Cinderella figure mistreated by two ugly aunts, made to do all the chores!

"You're not playing with us," snapped Mandy Biggerstaff, shoving Cindy so hard that she fell onto the playground. Mandy and her twin sister Candy pretended to help Cindy to her feet but as they did so they squeezed her arm so hard that she felt tears prickling her eyes.